English Foundation Plus

Activity Book C

Published by Collins
An imprint of HarperCollins*Publishers*
The News Building, 1 London Bridge Street,
London, SE1 9GF, UK

HarperCollins Publishers
Macken House, 39/40 Mayor Street Upper,
Dublin 1, D01 C9W8, Ireland

Browse the complete Collins catalogue at
www.collins.co.uk

British Library Cataloguing-in-Publication Data
A catalogue record for this publication is available from the British Library.

Author: Fiona Macgregor
Publisher: Elaine Higgleton
Product manager: Letitia Luff
Commissioning editor: Rachel Houghton
Edited by: Hannah Hirst-Dunton
Editorial management: Oriel Square
Cover designer: Kevin Robbins
Cover illustrations: Jouve India Pvt. Ltd.
Internal illustrations: Jouve India Pvt. Ltd.,
p 2, p 6t Manya Stojic, p 9–10 An Vrombaut,
p 15–19 John Gordon
Typesetter: Jouve India Pvt. Ltd.
Production controller: Lyndsey Rogers

Printed in India by Multivista Global Pvt. Ltd.

Acknowledgements

With thanks to all the kindergarten staff and their schools around the world who
have helped with the development of this course, by sharing insights and
commenting on and testing sample materials:

Calcutta International School: Sharmila Majumdar, Mrs Pratima Nayar, Preeti
Roychoudhury, Tinku Yadav, Lakshmi Khanna, Mousumi Guha, Radhika Dhanuka,
Archana Tiwari, Urmita Das; Gateway College (Sri Lanka): Kousala Benedict; Hawar
International School: Kareen Barakat, Shahla Mohammed, Jennah Hussain; Manthan
International School: Shalini Reddy; Monterey Pre-Primary: Adina Oram; Prometheus
School: Aneesha Sahni, Deepa Nanda; Pragyanam School: Monika Sachdev; Rosary
Sisters High School: Samar Sabat, Sireen Freij, Hiba Mousa; Solitaire Global School:
Devi Nimmagadda; United Charter Schools (UCS): Tabassum Murtaza and
staff; Vietnam Australia International School: Holly Simpson

The publishers wish to thank the following for permission to reproduce photographs.

(t – top, c – centre, b – bottom, r – right, l – left)

p 11t, p 13b fizkes/Shutterstock, p 11c1, p13t ALPA PROD/Shutterstock, p 11c2,
p13c1 Sahacha Nilkumhang/Shutterstock, p 11b, p 13c2 Kzenon/Shutterstock

The publishers gratefully acknowledge the permission granted to reproduce the
copyright material in this book. Every effort has been made to trace copyright
holders and to obtain their permission for the use of copyright material. The
publishers will gladly receive any information enabling them to rectify any
error or omission at the first opportunity.

Extracts from Collins Big Cat readers reprinted by permission of
HarperCollins*Publishers* Ltd

All © HarperCollins*Publishers*

MIX
Paper | Supporting
responsible forestry
FSC™ C007454

This book contains FSC™ certified paper and other controlled
sources to ensure responsible forest management.

For more information visit: www.harpercollins.co.uk/green

Match

snowy

sunny

foggy

windy

rainy

cloudy

Match the words to the pictures.

Date:

Draw

Monday	Tuesday
Wednesday	**Thursday**
Friday	**Weather I like**

Draw the weather on each day this week. In the last box, draw the weather you like.

Date:

3

Trace and match

M

T

W

F

S

s

m

t

w

f

Trace the letters. Write each letter between the lines.
Match each capital letter to a small letter.   Date:

Trace and say

rain

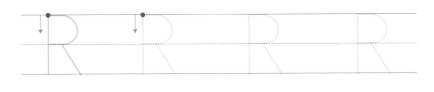

Trace the letter. Say the sound. Say the word.

Date:

Write

f o g

fr o g

c _ t

p _ t

Write the letter 'o' to complete each word.
Say the words.

Date:

Colour

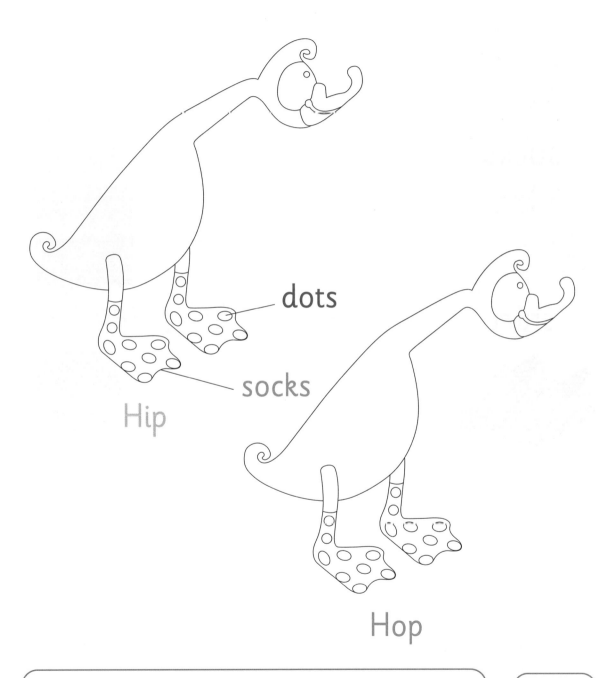

dots

socks

Hip

Hop

Colour Hip yellow. Colour Hop blue. Colour the dots red. Colour the rest of the socks green.

Date:

Match

socks

cloth

shirt

leather

shoes

wool

hat

straw

Match the thing to the material used to make it.

Date:

Find

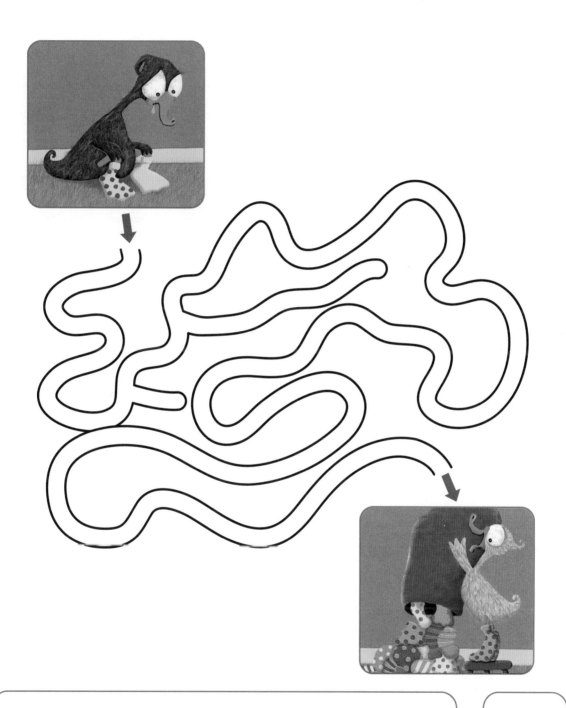

Follow the path to help Hop find his socks.

Date:

Trace and say

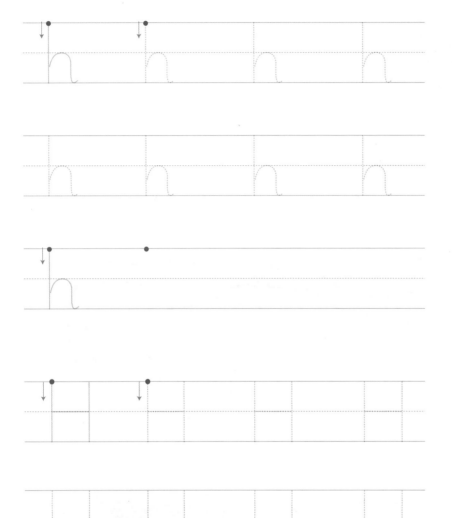

Hip

Trace the letter. Say the sound. Say the word.

Date:

Match

singer

pilot

driver

writer

Draw a line to match each word to a job.

Date:

Trace and say

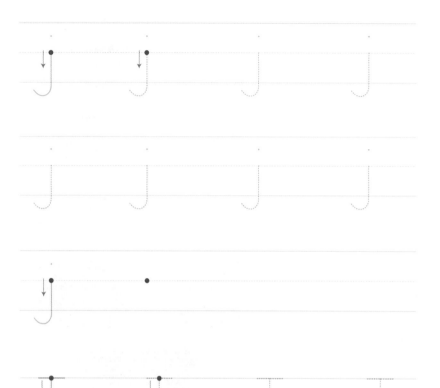

jam

Trace the letter. Say the sound. Say the word.

Date:

Trace and write

My job

My job

My job

My job

Trace the words. Say the job each person does.

Date:

Write

car

cat

v_n

h_t

m_n

Write the letter 'a' to complete each word.
Say the words.

Date:

Draw

My lunch

Draw your favourite lunch. Trace the words.

Date:

Circle

 Where's my  ?

apple

camera

sandwich

Where's my  ?

biscuit

camera

sandwich

Where's my 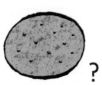 ?

lunch

farmer

biscuit

Where's my ?

apple

camera

sandwich

Circle the word that matches the picture in each sentence.

Date:

Say

on

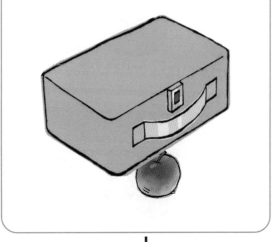

under

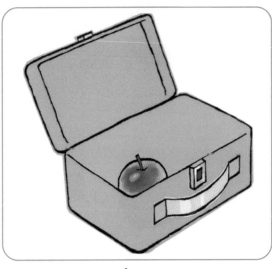

in

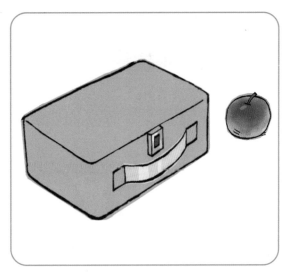

next to

Say where the apple is. Use this sentence:
'This apple is _____ the lunchbox.'

Date:

Find and circle

Follow the pattern in each line.
Circle what comes next.

Date:

Trace and say

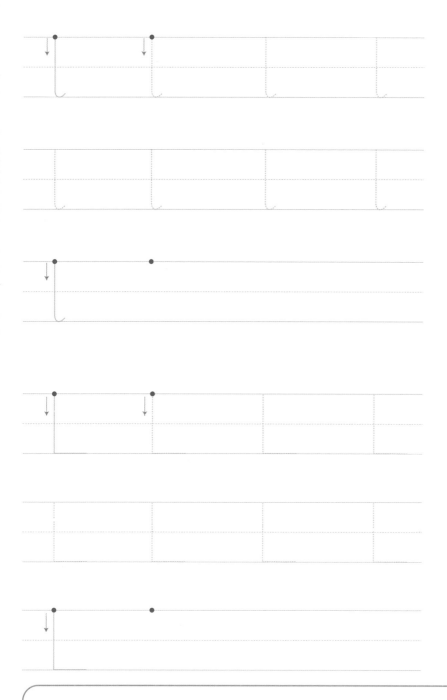

lunch

Trace the letter. Say the sound. Say the word.

Date:

Colour

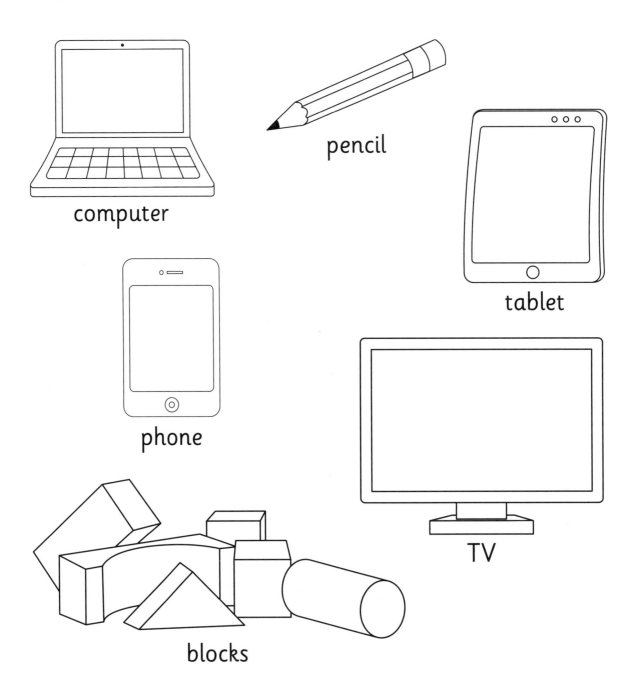

computer

pencil

tablet

phone

TV

blocks

Colour the things you can use.

Date:

Write

p _ n

b _ ll

h _ n

p _ g

n _ t

Write the letter 'e' to complete each word. Say the words.

Date:

Alphabet time

rabbit

snake

train

umbrella

Alongside structured phonics lessons, you may want to display and talk about one letter of the alphabet in an 'alphabet time' session each week.

Alphabet time

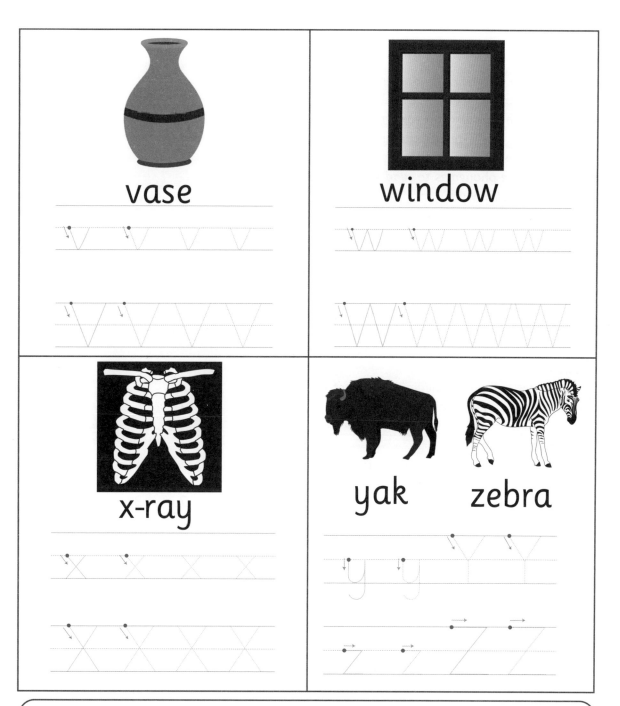

vase

window

x-ray

yak   zebra

Alongside structured phonics lessons, you may want to display and talk about one letter of the alphabet in an 'alphabet time' session each week.

Assessment record

_____ has achieved these English Foundation Plus Objectives:

Reading

R1 Develop an increasing awareness of sound structures in language	1	2	3
R2 Consolidate and develop early reading skills	1	2	3
R3 Recognise more letters of the English alphabet, and their corresponding sounds	1	2	3
R4 Begin to use phonemes to read single-syllable words with short vowels	1	2	3
Reading motor skills	1	2	3

Writing

W1 Consolidate and develop early writing skills	1	2	3
Writing motor skills	1	2	3

Speaking

S1 Be able to express oneself in a range of everyday situations	1	2	3
S2 Sentences and words: begin to segment and blend	1	2	3
Speaking developmental skills	1	2	3

Listening

L1 Know how to listen and respond appropriately in a range of everyday contexts	1	2	3
Listening developmental skills	1	2	3

> 1: Partially achieved
> 2: Achieved
> 3: Exceeded

Signed by teacher:
Signed by parent: Date: